MAKING CARS AT COWLEY

FROM MORRIS TO ROVER

GILLIAN BARDSLEY &
STEPHEN LAING

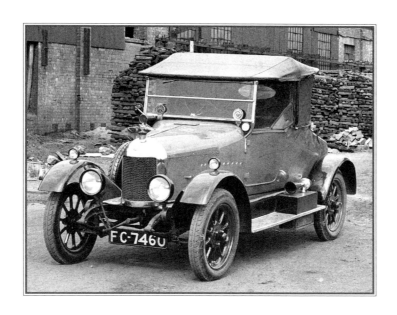

BRITISH MOTOR INDUSTRY HERITAGE TRUST

SUTTON PUBLISHING LIMITED

Sutton Publishing Limited
Phoenix Mill · Thrupp · Stroud
Gloucestershire · GL5 2BU

First published 1999

Published in association with the
British Motor Industry Heritage Trust

Copyright © Gillian Bardsley & Stephen
Laing, 1999

Half-title page photograph: Assembling
radiator cores (pp. 134–5); *title page
photograph*: A Bullnose car outside the
North Works, 1924 (p. 14); *below*: Wiring
and lamps being installed, 1929 (p. 42);
opposite: Mini production, 1959 (p. 138).

British Library Cataloguing in Publication Data
A catalogue record for this book is available from the
British Library.

ISBN 0-7509-2097-1

Typeset in 10.5/13.5 Photina.
Typesetting and origination by
Sutton Publishing Limited.
Printed in Great Britain by
Ebenezer Baylis, Worcester.

ACKNOWLEDGEMENTS

All the photographic material in this book is taken from the extensive archive collections
of the British Motor Industry Heritage Trust, which is located at the Heritage Motor
Centre, Banbury Road, Gaydon, Warwick, CV35 0BJ. The only exceptions to this are the
photographs on pp. 9 (bottom), 156 (top and bottom) and 157 (top and bottom), which
we would like to thank Mr Harry Turley for permission to use. Mr Turley has undertaken
to make a thorough photographic record of the demolition of the old factory and
redevelopment of the site and has kindly donated copies of his pictures to the archive.

The authors would also like to thank John Bacchus and Oliver White for their
generous and knowledgeable assistance with picture research and proof-reading.

MAKING CARS
AT COWLEY

This gold-plated model of the Morris Minor was presented to William Morris in 1957 to celebrate his eightieth birthday. Ironically, he never liked the new Morris Minor. Here we see him standing, with the model, by the desk in his office at the Nuffield Press building.

CONTENTS

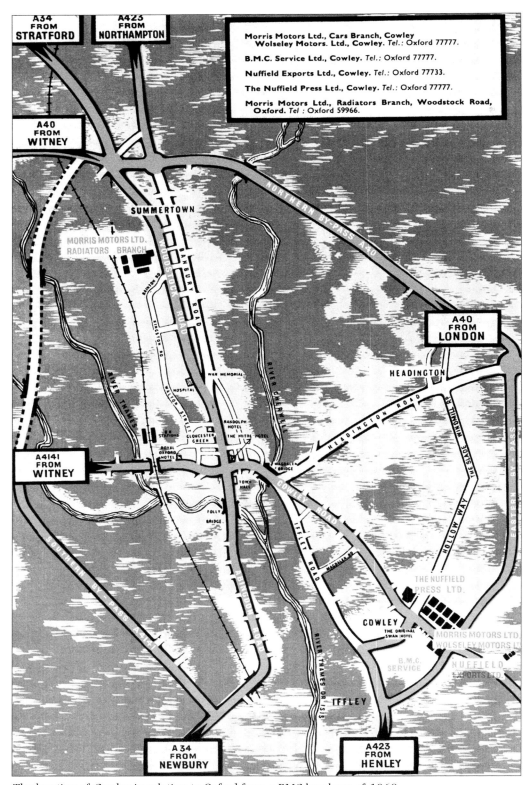

The location of Cowley in relation to Oxford from a BMC brochure of 1960.

INTRODUCTION

For more than eighty-five years Cowley has been the Oxford home of the automobile industry. From small but ambitious beginnings it grew to be one of the most important motor car factories in the world.

The Cowley plant was brought into being by one man, William Morris. In 1913 he converted a derelict military college on the outskirts of Oxford into a modest workshop to manufacture motor vehicles and opened the first chapter in one of the most extraordinary success stories of motoring history. His vision was to produce a motor vehicle of straightforward design, assembled from the best components and for a reasonable price, using all the latest techniques for efficient manufacturing.

By producing practical and affordable cars which sold all over the world, Morris widened the social scale of car ownership and thus helped to change the face of modern transport. It earned him a series of public honours, culminating in his elevation to the peerage as Lord Nuffield in 1938.

Despite all the changes which have transformed the organisation Morris created – expansion, merger with arch-rival Austin, the British Leyland days and the Rover era – Cowley remains one of the most up-to-date production sites and an essential part of the British motor industry.

Cowley has not just been a significant player in the development of the British motor industry; it has also played a key rôle in the history of Oxford itself, influencing the growth and nature of the city's economic and social life. Many thousands of people have passed through the gates of the various Morris factories or have been associated in some way or other with the motor trade it underpinned or the leisure activities it offered. Without it, Oxford today would be a very different place.

Chassis as far as the eye can see. These are 'Flatnose' Morris Cowleys being stored before removal to another part of the factory for the fitting of bodywork, 1927.

Laying foundations for the first phase of factory expansion at the Cowley site, 1919. The old Military College forms the backdrop to the building work eastwards from Oxford. The purpose was to erect a new body shop on the site of old allotments.

Seventy-five years later and the view returns. For the first time since the First World War, the redevelopment of the Cowley site in 1994 allowed this clear outlook onto the original Military College buildings.

An aerial view over the factory in 1921. The new buildings, used for body manufacture, were now well into operation and doubled the size of the Morris factory.

Looking westwards towards the centre of Oxford in 1966 during the days of the British Motor Corporation (BMC). In the foreground is the body plant, which began life as the Pressed Steel Company works. The factory now filled either side of both the Garsington Road and the Oxford Eastern Bypass. The original site is in the top right-hand corner of the photograph.

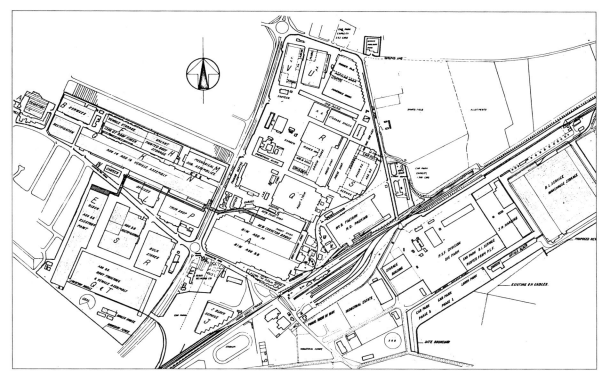

The extent of the factory in 1972 during the Austin Morris period of British Leyland. At this time, the factory employed one in seven of the population of Oxford.

1980s manufacturing techniques. This photograph of the assembly of a Rover 800 shows the engine and major subcomponents being fitted to a bodyshell from the underneath. This process is rather inelegantly known as the 'stuff-up' method.

Fifty years earlier; the marriage of body and chassis. The final stages of the construction of this 1934 Morris Ten involved the lowering of the steel body on to the completed chassis, both components having been manufactured separately.

The North Works in 1924. Looking beyond the Bullnose car reveals a pile of building materials, indicating that the expansion process was continuing apace. By the time this photograph was taken, annual production had increased to 18,000, three times what it had been only three years previously.

An unusual gathering in 1926. The contemporary description of this photograph reveals only that it shows the presentation of a silver casket to William Morris. Indeed, Morris is among the notables on the platform and the ceremony is most likely a gesture of his agents. The early Morris Oxford car and the gentleman with a film camera, both in the foreground, add to the atmosphere of the shot.

A typical street scene – along Oxford's High Street in 1928. Morris products are well represented in this view.

Sir William Morris with Leonard Lord in 1933. Lord was Morris' protégé, a talented engineer and businessman who was instrumental in the redevelopment of Cowley during the 1930s. He fell out with Morris and subsequently joined Austin. The two were to reunite in business in 1952 when Lord became chairman of the British Motor Corporation (BMC), which had resulted from the Austin–Morris merger.

A proud moment for Morris Motors: the one millionth Morris car reaches the end of the production line on 18 May 1939. Morris was the first British car company to manufacture one million cars, some seven years ahead of Austin.

The headlamp masks give away the period as being during the Second World War. A Morris Commercial lorry delivers new machinery to Cowley in 1944.

The Great Western Railway station at Cowley, built specifically to serve the factory workers.

The new conveyor, installed in 1954, stretching over what was to become the Oxford Eastern Bypass. The conveyor linked the North Works with the Pressed Steel body plant, obviating the need to transport new bodies the short distance by lorry.

Welcome to Cowley! Garsington Road in 1960 looking eastwards. In the distance are the Pressed Steel buildings, with the original factory site, by then home to Nuffield Press and the Apprentices' School, off to the left.

CHAPTER ONE

WILLIAM MORRIS, MAKING A START

The Morris premises at Longwall in 1907. The buildings were part of an extensive livery stables in Holywell Street, Oxford, backing on to the city walls. From there Morris not only conducted his business of cycle manufacture and cycle and motor car repair but built up a trade in garaging and maintaining the cars of Oxford undergraduates. This led on to Morris acquiring his own fleet of cars, which he hired out with drivers.

William Richard Morris was born in Worcestershire on 10 October 1877, but to Oxfordshire parents. His first employment was in the bicycle trade where he learnt his early skills. Typically, he soon decided to strike out on his own and, in 1893, set up his own business with a grand sum of £4 capital. His first repair business was operated from the back of his parents' house in James Street, Cowley. The front of the house soon became a showroom, selling accessories and his own design of bicycle.

Before too long Morris had outgrown his parents' home and took premises at 48 High Street, using a second building at 1 Queens Lane for storage and repairs. His interest naturally turned to motor power and, in 1902, he formed his first partnership with Joseph Cooper to provide more capital for expansion into the field of motorcycles. Using the High Street building as a headquarters, the new business took on some disused livery stables at Longwall but disagreements over production methods (Morris was already thinking of batch production) meant the partnership was short-lived. A further partnership in 1903, the Oxford Automobile and Cycle Agency, drew Morris into the motor car repair and sales business but this collapsed after only a year and led Morris to vow that he would keep control of his own businesses from then on.

The garage at Longwall quickly gained a reputation for good quality of service and Morris was able to expand, building new premises on the same site in 1910 that were officially named 'The Morris Garages'. Expansion at Longwall had given Morris the impetus to design his own car to challenge the Ford Model T, which had become the car to beat in the automobile markets of Britain and the whole world. Morris fully embraced Ford's advanced methods of production and produced a light car, at a low price, giving priority to the principles of reliability and low running costs.

The original company, set up in 1912, was named WRM Motors and its first product was the Morris Oxford, a two-seater 8.9 hp car advertised at a price of £165. Morris had realised that he could produce the best car by sourcing the components from individual suppliers rather than manufacturing everything himself. This method of getting the choicest parts at the best value was to underpin his business ethic throughout his career.

Longwall was not big enough to produce cars on a mass scale. Morris had been fortunate to secure an order from Gordon Stewart of London for 400 cars on the basis of a blueprint, before a single car had been produced. This prompted him to find larger premises and he settled on a property in Temple Cowley, a disused Military College that had previously been the Hurst's Grammar School. The conversion of this building was the first step towards establishing Cowley as the base for what would become a network of Morris factories known collectively as the 'Nuffield' organisation. Meanwhile, The Morris Garages at Longwall continued as William Morris' personal business, acting as a Morris distributor and service centre.

In the first year of production 393 cars were produced, followed by another 907 the next year. Unfortunately the year happened to be 1914 and war loomed large. William Morris was extremely concerned. His fledging motor car company was at risk of failing from the restrictions of wartime. Unlike companies with an engineering foundation, WRM Motors was based on assembly. The large amount of funds tied up in stock, with which Morris could do little, threatened the business.

Orders for the production of hand grenades and Stokes bomb cases could not make up for lost car production and profit turned to loss.

It was the application of Morris' production methods to munitions that began to win him favours. His orderly approach to manufacture led to his involvement with the various committees that advised on war production. In 1916, while discussing new devices, mine sinkers were considered. Only 40 per week could be made using traditional methods. Morris promised 250 and secured a contract. By employing his methods of sub-contracting the individual component manufacture and concentrating on assembly, Morris was able to reach a peak weekly output of 2,000. Profits returned to Cowley and Morris earned an OBE.

William Morris and his family in 1896. He is standing with his sister Alice; his mother Emily, father Frederick and sister Emily are sitting in front.

William Morris in 1909 at the wheel of one of his hire cars.

William Morris' great passion was for cycling. Not only was his first business that of cycle maker but he was a keen racing cyclist as well. He won many racing medals in Oxfordshire, Berkshire and Buckinghamshire, most notably in 1900 when he secured seven championships riding cycles built by his own hand. In 1904 he was challenged to race again after three years free from competition, in order to defend the trophies he had won from the now defunct East Oxford and Oxonian Cycling Clubs. With barely two weeks' notice and reluctantly riding a machine he had not made himself, Morris claimed the trophies again, this time permanently.

One week's production of the Morris Oxford, lined up outside the original Cowley factory in 1913.

Opposite, above: In 1903 Morris went into partnership with an Oxford businessman and an undergraduate at Christ Church. Morris was to be works manager of the enterprise, which became known as the Oxford Automobile and Cycle Agency. Its purpose was to build and repair cycles and motor cycles as well as trade in motor cars. A showroom was located in George Street with workshops in New Street. The partnership was short-lived, the Agency going bankrupt in 1904. Here the staff of the Agency sit for a photograph in 1903. Morris is in the centre.

Below: The first Morris car, the Morris Oxford, in 1912. On the left at the front of the car is Joseph Cooper with whom, in 1902, Morris had formed his first business partnership making and repairing cycles and motor cycles.

The inadequacies of the tram service in Oxford led William Morris to apply for a licence to operate a bus service in 1913. His application was ignored by the City Council, so he decided to start a service regardless, using a fleet of six Daimler buses. They were an immediate success and the trams were shunned by the travelling public. The tram companies retaliated by introducing a bus service but these were likewise unfrequented.

MORRIS DANCING AT OXFORD.

Public opinion forced the City Council to compromise and twelve licences were issued to Morris and twelve to the tram companies. Having proved his point, Morris arranged to sell his licences to the tram companies, satisfied that he had forced an improvement in the city's public transport. A Segar cartoon depicts the city councillors dancing to Morris' tune over the omnibus affair. Morris' legal advisor, Mr Grey, is on the right, looking from his office on one side of St Aldates to the Town Clerk's office on the other.

The Morris-Oxford Light Car.

1914   **1914**

Manufacturers: **W.R.M. MOTORS, LTD.,**

Codes: A1 A.B.C. (4th & 5th)
Engineering (2nd edition) Liebers, Western Union.

THE COWLEY MOTOR WORKS,
COWLEY, - near OXFORD.

Telegrams and Cables:
" VOITURETTE, COWLEY—OXON."

Wholesale and Shipping Agent:
W. H. M. BURGESS,
40 GLASSHOUSE STREET, LONDON, W.

Telephone: **590** *Oxford.*

1

The front cover from an early brochure for the Morris Oxford Light Car. The original motor company was called 'WRM Motors', these being Morris' initials.

An illustration from a 1914 Morris Oxford brochure showing the car competing in a hill-climb. William Morris competed in the Caerphilly hill-climb in 1913 in one of his own cars, coming sixth. In that year Morris Oxfords came first and second in the Irondown hill-climb and also came first, second and third in the Oxfordshire Motor Club annual hill-climb.

Dispatch Note No. ....

Customers' Cars are driven by our Staff only at Customers' own Risk and Responsibility.

Telephone Number: 590 Oxford.   Telegraphic Address: "VOITURETTE," COWLEY—OXON.

Bought of W.R.M. MOTORS Ltd.,

Reg. Offices: THE COWLEY MOTOR WORKS,

Manufacturers of the
"Morris-Oxford" and "Morris-Cowley" Light Cars.

COWLEY,

Near OXFORD.

Clayton Wright, Esq.,   29th March, 1916.

C/o Messrs Lucas, Ltd., Birmingham.

In all correspondence respecting this Invoice please quote Number.

1 Morris Cowley Limousine No. 3359.

Complete to Catalogue Specification,		257	5	0
Less 20%		51	9	0
		205	16	0
Extra for Rounded Corners to Back Part of Body,		2	18	6
" " Ventilators to Scuttle Dash,			15	9
" " Special Mudguards and Fittings,		6	11	6
" " Tray for Tools and Step Board,		1	12	6
" " "Perry" Type Dickey Seat,		3	15	0
" " Special Antique Leather Upholstery,		8	8	0
" " Child's Seat inside,		2	9	6
" " Silk Blinds with Spring Rollers,		2	0	6
" " Lock to Door			7	6
" " Hall Flap in Windscreen		1	11	6
" " Aluminium on Running Boards,			16	6
" " 4 Grooved Tyres,		1	6	0
" " 6th Wheel		1	0	0
" " 6th Inner Tube			11	1
		239	12	10

Less Lighting Set,	£10-11-6			
" Allowance for non-supply of 5th Plain Cover,	1- 9-0			
" Bulb Horn	7-6	12	8	0
Nett	£227	4	10

Introduced in 1915, the Morris Cowley could be fitted with a four-seater or a two-seater body while the Oxford only came as a two-seater. The Cowley was £10 cheaper to boot. It was fitted with an American engine, built by the Continental Motor Manufacturing Company of Detroit and became known as the 'Continental Cowley'. The body style was, however, thoroughly British and a number of chassis were fitted with special bodies. This invoice is for one such luxurious Cowley, supplied to Clayton Wright of the Joseph Lucas Company, manufacturers of electrical components.

During the First World War, Morris turned to munitions production. Morris made the production of mine sinkers his own, having realised that his principles of car assembly could be translated to wartime needs. Here a train load of sinkers departs from Cowley in 1917.

From 1914 onwards most of the factory was given over to munitions production, although car production continued at a trickle. This 1917 view shows equipment and components for munitions assembly.

Morris did not just make mine sinkers, he transported them as well using vehicles like this fleet of decorated 'Trench Warfare' trucks, seen here on parade in 1918 during victory celebrations. Most of the drivers were women, more than 400 of whom had been engaged in war work at Morris.

Peace returns – factory workers listen to the factory band during Armistice Day celebrations in 1918.

By 1919, the paraphernalia of war production had been cleared away. This view in August of that year shows that cars were once again being made in earnest.

CHAPTER TWO

THE MOVE TO
MASS PRODUCTION

*William Morris (on the left) stands with Miles Thomas (on the right) in front of a 1924
Morris Oxford that had run from Land's End to John O' Groats without stopping the engine.*

Once the hostilities of the First World War were ended the company was renamed Morris Motors Ltd and entered a new phase in its development. During the war years, Morris had only been able to produce a trickle of cars, some 1,500 up to 1919. The cessation of munitions manufacture meant that much of the machinery brought in had to be returned. This might have been adjudged to be detrimental to the post-war operation but in many ways turned out to be just what Cowley needed.

Before the war, the manufacture of the Morris Oxford was constrained by the layout of the Military College. The building had three storeys. On the ground floor, machining, drilling and any preparation work was undertaken. The chassis components were moved up to the next level, where they were laid out in batches on the floor. Engines were lifted into the chassis and then the axles and other components fitted. Workers moved along the line of cars to fit the parts. When complete, the chassis were moved to the top level, where the bodies were mounted and the complete cars stored.

Just before the war, a new steel structure was constructed in the centre courtyard of the old college, on what was once the parade ground. This allowed the main assembly to be transferred out of the original building and the new shops were laid out for flow production. Once the chassis could accept them, wheels were attached and the chassis moved from one station to the next as each component was fitted. So the practice was turned around and instead of the workers moving to the assembly, now the assembly moved to them as they stayed at their fixed stations.

The stocks of parts that had counted against Cowley before the war, allowed it to restart production almost immediately after peace was declared. At the same time the new production lines helped Morris to produce cars quickly and re-establish its name in the market.

In late 1920 and early 1921 Cowley faced another dilemma. There was an unexpected slump in the economy and the motor industry, selling a product with a high premium, suffered badly. The factory's output dropped from over 250 per week in September 1920 down to 74 per week the following January. Morris was determined not to stop manufacture completely and used the goodwill of his suppliers to get parts in advance of payment on the understanding that he would find a way to sell his cars. He also negotiated a reduction in the margin that his distributors got from their sales. Finally, he made the biggest and possibly bravest move of all – he cut his car prices. The price of a four-seater Cowley was lowered by £100, a reduction of 25 per cent.

The result was almost immediate. Ahead of its rivals, Morris Motors' sales rose again, regaining their previous level. Morris also planned expansion at Cowley to reduce manufacturing costs even further. In 1921/2 the first wave of new buildings was constructed on the site of some allotments across the road from the Military College. 'B' block, a six-bay shed, was the first of the North Works buildings and housed the body shop. 'C' block followed soon after and took vehicle assembly away from the Military College. The shop was purpose-built for flow production, the cars moving along stations as they were constructed. Other buildings were erected and by 1926 the works covered more than 40 acres. By 1927, the workforce had risen to 5,000 and this figure stayed roughly constant up to the Second World War. More expansion followed. 'P' block, a repair shop, was completed in 1929, bringing the total works size to over 80 acres.

By the early 1930s, the assembly lines at Cowley had become outmoded. Leonard Lord had impressed William Morris with the work he had done at his engine factory and in 1933 Lord was given the task of reorganising Cowley's production areas. He began by introducing moving assembly lines, obviating the need for chassis to be manually rolled along the track on slave wheels. In the main assembly 'C' block, the number of lines was increased by three to five. Chassis were delivered to storage lines, from which they were transported to the assembly lines as required. Components were distributed by overhead crane from a central platform. Even the wheel conveyor was able to distinguish the different sized wheels and deliver them via chutes to the appropriate model line.

A transverse conveyor took the completed chassis to the body mounting area. Blocks 'G' and 'K' were amalgamated to provide an integrated body mounting, trimming, finishing and paint shop. Bodies started at one end, chassis at the other. Bodies travelled in one direction to be painted on the lower half and, on returning, were painted on the upper half. They were then trimmed and taken by overhead conveyor to the middle point of the line and lowered onto the chassis. Once complete, the cars went to the despatch department where they were filled with oil and petrol using fast-delivery pumps. A single day's stock of 400 cars could be stored in the department.

Also formed in the early 1930s was the Morris Industrial Exports department to co-ordinate exports for the growing network of Morris companies. A 50,000 square foot building was put up next to the sidings close to Cowley railway station.

The face of Cowley in 1928. By now Morris had fully adopted mass production techniques, cars being moved down a track and built up at stations of particular components to minimise the movement of parts.

Installing an engine in 1926. If we compare this view with the previous photograph it is apparent that track production methods were still being developed.

Bullnoses as far as the eye can see in 1926. These completed chassis have been fitted with the trademark 'Bullnose' radiator, which was made by the Osberton Radiator Company of Oxford.

Two views of the paint shop in the 'C' block of North Works. Assembled chassis were manoeuvred off the chassis sub-assembly line onto turntables . . .

. . . where they were manipulated into one of four paint spray booths.

Once in the spray booth, two men could spray a complete chassis in two minutes. The chassis was held in a cradle and rotated, making each part accessible.

Once painted, the chassis were moved through drying kilns, pulled along by a system of chains and ratchets. When they had emerged from the kiln, the steering wheels were attached. Steering wheels awaiting fitment can be seen hanging at the end of the kilns.

For the journey along the track, the cars were fitted with 'slave' wheels. These were disc wheels used only to move the car around, the correct wheels being fitted at the end of the assembly line.

Once the chassis had been completed and the front wings attached, electrical components were fitted. In this 1929 view, wiring and lamps are being installed on the car.

Installation of certain chassis components required extra height on the line. At the relevant stations, cars could be lifted off the line by hydraulic jacks to allow work and then dropped back on the line before moving off to the next area. Note the wooden block to get that extra bit of height to suit the assembler.

Not every job was carried out directly on the track. In 1926 electrical equipment was still fitted in a separate shop after the correct wheels and tyres had been attached.

Women were only employed in any numbers from 1915 onwards when, as in other industries, they were drafted in to replace the men who were being called up after the introduction of conscription. At Cowley they were engaged on small component assembly, as in this view where they are gauging axle components.

On a carousel. The rear axle and torque tube assembly lines were kept apart, with separate differential gear and propeller shaft lines converging on the torque tube line. Both ended in this 'start stand', which held the torque tube in place while the rear axle was bolted onto it. Notice also, in the background, the workers' bicycles leaning against the wall.

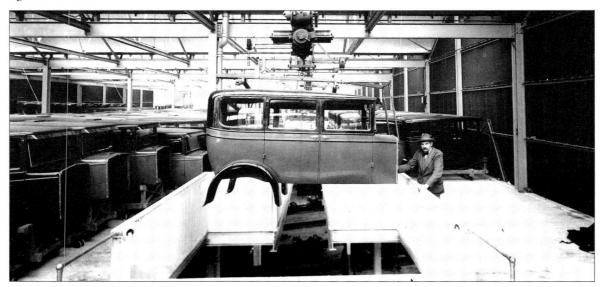

Bodies were constructed on separate lines from the chassis. Once complete, they were stored on the top floor until the time came for them to be lowered to the factory floor and attached to the waiting chassis.

Chassis were moved across from 'C' block in convoys of five or so, towed by the first chassis and delivered to 'G' block. Once in the body mounting shop, bodies were dropped down onto the chassis by means of an overhead crane.

The body stores in 1926. Completed and partially completed cars stand awaiting attention.

The mounting department in 1930 where Morris Oxford two- and four-seaters are being trimmed and finished. The sign above outlines the work being carried out: 'fitting of the rear screen, bonnet, ventilator and lino to foot and bottom board and attaching the bonnet beading'.

At the end of the line: the final chassis line for Morris Minors and Oxfords in 1933.

When complete, the cars were given a road test. Fitted with its trade plates, this car is being filled with petrol ready for a run.

It was not only complete cars that were tested on the road; from time to time chassis were also tried out with the drivers perched on a crude soap box.

From the early 1920s, the Morris factory continued to grow. The North Works, sited opposite the original factory buildings, was almost constantly being expanded during that time and the total area covered by the works was over 80 acres by the time this shot was taken in 1930. It is amusing to note that the horse and cart was still very much a part of the building trade, even when constructing a motor factory!

The Subscription List will close on or before the 14th day of July, 1926.

MORRIS MOTORS (1926) LIMITED

(Incorporated under the Companies Acts, 1908 to 1917.)

AUTHORISED CAPITAL:

3,000,000 Seven and a-Half per Cent. Cumulative Preference Shares of £1 each	- - - - - -	£3,000,000
2,000,000 Ordinary Shares of £1 each	- - -	£2,000,000

ISSUE OF

3,000,000 Seven and a-Half per Cent. Cumulative Preference Shares of £1 each at par.

PAYABLE:—

On Application - - - - -	2s. 6d.
On Allotment - - - -	7s. 6d.
On the 16th day of August, 1926 -	5s. 0d.
On the 16th day of September, 1926 -	5s. 0d.
	£1 0s. 0d.

The Preference Shares will entitle the holders to receive out of the profits available for distribution a fixed Cumulative Preferential Dividend of 7½ per cent. per annum, and to priority both as regards capital and dividend over the other shares of the Company, but to no further participation in profits or assets.

The Preference Shares will rank for a full Three months' Dividend to the 30th September, 1926.

It is intended to pay this dividend on the 30th October, 1926, and to pay subsequent dividends on the Preference Shares half-yearly, on the 31st day of March and the 30th day of September.

The Company will set aside to a Reserve Fund at least 25 per cent. of the balance of the net profits of each year remaining after payment of the fixed dividend on the Preference Shares until the Reserve Fund amounts to not less than £1,000,000.

The Articles of Association will be altered to provide that no shares ranking in priority to or *pari passu* with the Preference Shares will be issued without the sanction of an Extraordinary Resolution of the holders of the Preference Shares.

The whole of the 2,000,000 Ordinary Shares will be issued credited as fully paid to the Vendors as part of the Purchase consideration.

Directors.

WILLIAM RICHARD MORRIS, Manor House, Cowley, Oxford, Governing Director of Morris Motors Limited and its Associated Companies (Chairman and Managing Director).

EDGAR HANSCOMB BLAKE, 122, Banbury Road, Oxford, Deputy Governing Director of Morris Motors Limited and its Associated Companies (Vice-Chairman and Deputy Managing Director).

WILLIAM HENRY FULFORD, Manor House, Aston-le-Walls, Northants, General Manager of Hollick & Pratt Limited, Coventry.

HUGH WORDSWORTH GREY, Greenheys, Boars Hill, Berks, Sales Manager, Cowley Works, Oxford.

HANS LANDSTAD, 102, Divinity Road, Oxford, General Works Manager, Cowley Works, Oxford.

ARTHUR ALBERT ROWSE, Wootton, Berks, Production Manager, Cowley Works, Oxford.

HAROLD ALFRED RYDER, 368, Woodstock Road, Oxford, General Manager, Radiator Works, Oxford.

FRANK GEORGE WOOLLARD, 5, Dalton Road, Coventry, General Manager, Engines Works, Coventry.

HENRY WILLIAM YOUNG, West End, Witney, Oxon, General Works Engineer, Cowley Works, Oxford.

Bankers.

BARCLAYS BANK LIMITED, Head Office, 54, Lombard Street, London, E.C.3, and Branches.

Brokers.

LAING & CRUICKSHANK, 6, Austin Friars, London, E.C.2.

FYSHE & HORTON, 3, Temple Row West and Stock Exchange, Birmingham.

Solicitors.

ANDREW WALSH & BARTRAM, 116, St. Aldate's Street, Oxford.

ASHURST, MORRIS, CRISP & CO., 17, Throgmorton Avenue, London, E.C.2.

Consulting Accountants.

PRICE, WATERHOUSE & CO., Chartered Accountants, 3, Frederick's Place, Old Jewry, London, E.C.2

Auditors.

THORNTON & THORNTON, Chartered Accountants, Moorgate Station Chambers, London, E.C.2, and 3 & 4, King Edward Street, Oxford.

Secretary and Registered Office.

S. G. K. SMALLBONE, Cowley, Oxon.

BARCLAYS BANK LIMITED, Head Office, 54, Lombard Street, London, E.C.3, and Branches,
THE UNION BANK OF MANCHESTER LIMITED, Head Office, York Street, Manchester, and Branches, and
THE BRITISH LINEN BANK, Head Office, 38, St. Andrew Square, Edinburgh, and Branches
are authorised as Bankers for and on behalf of the Company to receive Applications for the Seven and a-Half per Cent. Cumulative Preference Shares now offered for subscription.

On 29 June 1926 a new public company was registered in the name of Morris Motors (1926) Ltd. The company acquired the assets of Morris Motors Ltd, Osberton Radiators Ltd and Hollick and Pratt Ltd. Funds were provided by £2 million in Ordinary shares and £3 million in Preference shares with fixed interest. Morris retained control by becoming the sole Ordinary shareholder. This is the prospectus for the share issue.

HRH The Prince of Wales visits Cowley on 24 May 1927. The Prince chats to a factory worker – former Company Sergeant Major Brooks VC. Meanwhile, William Morris, in the foreground with his hat tilted casually back, is in discussion with another of his employees.

The world-wide export market was essential to Morris and visiting dignitaries were often welcomed to the factory. In this 1928 picture, a party from the African Gold Coast pose with Miles Thomas for a photograph.

More than any other, the Ford company's production methods were the rôle model for William Morris. Yet, when Henry Ford (in the centre of the picture) visited Cowley in 1928, Morris was not there to greet him, choosing instead to meet him the next day in London.

Leaving for home in 1930. The bicycle was still the standard method of transport for the workforce. More than 10,000 worked for the Morris group of companies by 1930 and over half were employed at Cowley.

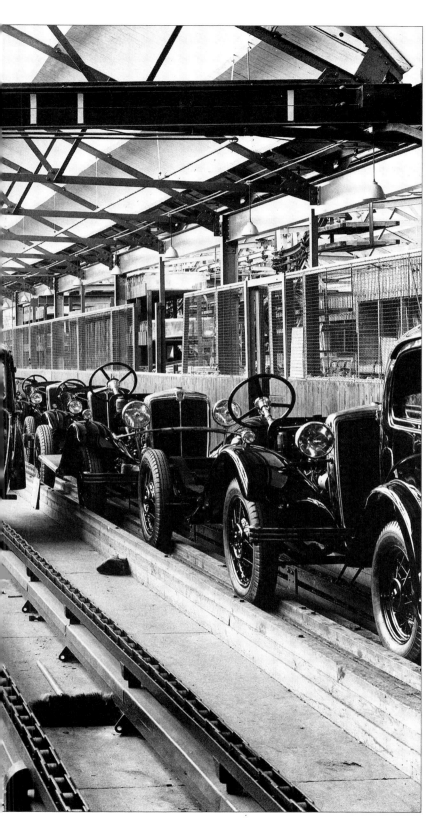

The Morris Eight line in 1934. The system for moving bodies along can be easily seen.

Even the delivery of wheels to the track was done mechanically, eliminating the need for piles of wheels being stacked next to the line.

Morris stands with Leonard Lord to the left on the occasion of the 100,000th Morris Eight to be produced. The car rolled out of the factory in 1936.

As well as the straightforward road tests, cars were subjected to many other trials such as this water spray test on an Eight Series E in 1939.

Nor did the car have to leave the factory any more for the road test. Here, a Morris Eight is tested on the rolling road. The machine in the background, a dynamometer, measures whether the performance of the car comes up to specification.

A new production line installed in 1938. Cars were no longer rolled along a track on their wheels but pulled along by a chain on a continuously moving line. Components were brought in by overhead conveyors and were dropped down at exactly the right spot on the

A page from the 1935 factory visitors' book – a most interesting entry in the form of a caricature by the Scottish entertainer Harry Lauder.

CHAPTER THREE

THE COACHBUILDING REVOLUTION

A fine example of the finished coachbuilt body – a 1925 four-seater Oxford, as elegant as its new owners.

In the 1920s the process of building bodies was the most labour intensive part of the production of a motor car. Construction was done by traditional coachbuilding methods, which involved building up a wooden frame, panelling with metal, painting and finishing. All these jobs were done by skilled teams of workers and did not lend themselves to flow production.

On one of his trips to America, William Morris was introduced to Edward G. Budd of Philadelphia. Budd had revolutionised the body-building process in the American motor industry by introducing the all-steel body. The whole structure of the body was built up by pressed steel panels, welded together to make a single body unit.

Morris was immediately attracted to the idea, which he recognised to be the final piece of the flow production jigsaw. He decided to become involved in a joint venture with the Budd Company and bankers, J. Henry Schroeder and Co. The Pressed Steel Company was established in 1926 making the large investment of £120,000 in Budd's dies and tools.

It was natural to build the new factory adjacent to the Cowley works and the main assembly building for Pressed Steel was sited on the corner of Garsington Road and Poplar Road (later to become the Oxford Eastern Bypass), to the east of the Morris Motors works. The factory building was of massive size, covering some 10 acres and accommodating more than 60 steel presses.

Morris was eager to see a quick return for the large investment in the new tools but was initially frustrated by teething problems with the new techniques and workers unfamiliar with them. The first pressings failed from buckling, rippling and burst steel. It was intended that the 1927 Morris model range should have all-steel bodies, but because of the production problems composite coachwork was fitted. Things were soon turned around, however, and before too long the factory was able to turn out bodies efficiently and speedily.

The beauty of the process was in the handling of materials. While areas were separated according to the production of bodies for different motor companies, good planning allowed the flow of raw material from one side of the factory to complete bodies on the other.

Unfortunately, the fact that Morris Motors had an interest in the ownership of Pressed Steel began to affect business. Orders from other motor companies were hard to come by while other pressings companies were reluctant to quote for Morris Motors work. In 1930 Morris Motors therefore relinquished its shares in Pressed Steel and the company went on to flourish, making presswork for many manufacturers including Hillman, Austin, Jaguar, Rover, Rolls-Royce and Standard.

In the late 1930s the Pressed Steel site was expanded further. A new paint shop was constructed and connected to the main assembly building by an overhead conveyor. A canteen and office was constructed adjacent to the Oxford Eastern Bypass, the office clock tower of which is still a central feature of today's Rover plant.

Pressed Steel was to remain an independent company until 1965 when merger with the British Motor Corporation brought it back into the same fold as its old partner, Morris Motors.

The late 1920s and early 1930s were a period of transition between the body made by traditional coachbuilding methods and the newer all-steel pressed body. In the coachbuilding process, wood was still an essential material and many factories contained a sawmill such as the one pictured here at Cowley in 1933.

Traditionally, bodies were built up by hand, using a basic wooden frame structure often made of ash. This 1929 view shows the construction of Minor saloon bodies. The bodies were then covered with hand-beaten metal panels, as can be seen on some of the cars in the background.

The North Works 'B' block body shop was built in 1921/2. The high number of people required by the older methods of body building can clearly be seen. Coachbuilders worked in 'gangs' of four or five.

Finished bodies were mounted on trestles while they were trimmed and small components added. On the right-hand side of the photograph, bodies awaiting attention are stacked on their bulkhead ends.

It was important to ensure that the bodies were accurately put together. Setting up the body jig was a complicated and skilled process.

Preparing panels for finishing was also very labour intensive. Many hours were consumed in rubbing down and finishing bodywork.

Another view of the body shop, this time in 1926, showing the construction of saloon bodies. Although there is no moving track and each body is being constructed on a fixed base, an attempt to introduce the principle of organised workflow to body manufacture has been made.

P·S·C "one-piece" bodies now adopted for the newest cars

PRESSED STEEL COMPANY
OXFORD

Coachbuilding represented a brake on the development of full mass-production methods because it was by its nature so labour intensive and time consuming. The introduction of the new pressed steel technique was therefore a major advance in the industry. This is an advertisement for the revolutionary Pressed Steel Company, pinned on the drawing board in 1930.

The Pressed Steel Company constructed its factory to the east side of what is now the Oxford Eastern Bypass, adjacent to the Morris Works. This view, taken in the latter part of 1926, shows the installation of the massive presses. Many of the machines and the initial batches of raw material were shipped over directly from the Budd Company of Philadelphia. The presses were moved into place using skilled men, many of whom had come from the ship industry.

The factory in 1938. The large presses made the production of more complicated shapes, like wings, much easier and quicker.

The immense size of the equipment is well illustrated by the tiny figures of the two operators. Working at Pressed Steel was often a dangerous job. Only a few of the sixty or so presses had guards and the working environment was invariably dirty.

A major advantage of the all-steel body was that a vast number of panels could be stamped out in a short space of time in contrast to the time-consuming process of hand-beating and fitting individual panels over wooden frames.

The finished article, a four-door Pressed Steel body.

The Pressed Steel works also had its own paint shop. When a body left the works it was a complete unit ready to mount on the awaiting mechanical assembly.

The nature of the process meant that small adjustments had to be made to the bodies as they travelled along the line. Here a jack is used to tweak the body so that the doors hang and close properly.

Sometimes it was still necessary, as part of the finishing process, to use a hand wheeling machine to ensure the correct curvature of the panel.

Another production technique that came with the all-steel body was electric welding. It gave an advantage in terms of speed and repeatability where spot welds every few inches were all that was required.

The trim shop at Pressed Steel in 1934. After the First World War, women mostly disappeared from the factory floor. The trim shop was the main production area where one could still find them.

The all-steel body facilitated development of the monocoque, cars being constructed with no separate chassis, just a bodyshell containing the mechanical components. Here we see the assembly line in 1939 with components being welded together using hand-held welding guns that were suspended from overhead rails.

CHAPTER FOUR

A GIFT FOR PUBLICITY

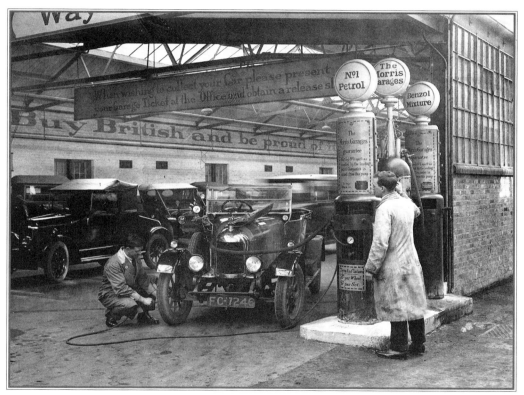

Keeping the customer happy, 1923 – Morris Garages offered a full range of customer services including tyre inflation at a cost of 2d for a single tyre or 6d for all four. While waiting, the owner could muse on the sentiment 'Buy British and be proud of it'.

William Morris claimed to shun the advertising media, boasting that he had never spent even a halfpenny on advertising between 1912 and 1918, as the cars had sold themselves! In reality, he showed a gift for publicity from the very beginning. At the very start of his business life he advertised his cycle business in Kelly's Directory of Oxford and promoted his own name by his success as a racing cyclist.

When he moved into motor manufacture he rarely missed a promotional opportunity. In 1912, for example, he provided motor dealers with catalogues to encourage them to stock Morris cars. It was in the early 1920s, however, that sales promotion began in earnest. Morris realised that cheerful owners were the best advertisement for the product. By looking after them and making them feel part of the company, he could count on them spreading a favourable message about the cars. In 1924 the first issue of the *Morris Owner* was published. Under the auspices of Miles Thomas, a young journalist who had impressed William Morris (no mean task), the *Morris Owner* was the first British motor industry journal to be available commercially. It extolled the product while also giving motoring advice and recounting holiday tales. The magazine continued until 1951 and was much copied by rival firms. Millions of copies were circulated, even before the war.

To publish this new journal and to meet the growing requirement for company publications, the Morris Oxford Press was established in 1925 (and renamed Nuffield Press in 1942) to produce and print Morris material. It was set up in the original part of the Cowley factory, the old Military College buildings, where Lord Nuffield still kept his office. The Nuffield Press continues publishing today.

Another popular way of promoting the product was to tell tales of its durability. One of the more famous tales was born of Lord Northcliffe's interest in the British motor car. Northcliffe was the proprietor of the *Daily Mail* and arranged for his motoring correspondent, John Prioleau, to take a 1920 Morris Oxford two-seater on a tour of Europe and Mediterranean. Each of the 7,000 miles covered in the six-month tour, which began in 1920, was serialised in the newspaper and the lively diary provided Morris with invaluable free advertising.

The process of making the motor car was always of interest to the public. Every opportunity was used to show of the latest production techniques being practised at Cowley. Modern technology was perceived to mean the best product. Cowley established its own film unit, which spent a great deal of its time recording every aspect of factory life. These films were turned into short documentaries used to keep the factory worker, the distributor and customer alike up to date with the latest developments at Cowley. The film unit also made promotional films for Morris products and William Morris was a frequent player in this celluloid advertising. The department had the most modern film equipment and a fleet of vans to carry the crews to the locations.

The Morris Garages showroom was known for its elegant window displays. This illuminating 1929 display for Exide batteries shows the elaborate advertising techniques employed, complete with a £1,000 limerick competition!

In 1932 Morris Garages opened a new showroom at St Aldates, Oxford, at a cost of £80,000, which was to become the flagship Morris dealership. Morris Garages was retained as William Morris' personal business even after the public flotation of Morris Motors in 1926. This view was taken in 1950.

Inside a typical showroom the customer could browse through Morris brochures in well-appointed surroundings. This gentleman would have to pay £260 for an Oxford two-seater and £195 for a Cowley four-seater in 1924.

Morris offered a range of signs to its distributors, from the illuminated Bullnose radiator to the showroom barometer.

One of the more unusual accessories for a Morris car was the Morris Motor House, introduced in 1926. There were two models of these prefabricated garages, one for the Cowley at £15 15s 0d and a slightly larger version for the Oxford at £17 0s 0d.

In 1924 William Morris launched a journal called the *Morris Owner*, in order to promote Morris cars to his customers. In August 1925 the Morris Oxford Press (later Nuffield Press) was formed to print the *Morris Owner* as well as other company publications.

Typesetting Morris publications at the Morris Oxford Press in 1938.

Printing presses in 1938.

Collating 1929 publications on the endless band conveyor.

The ideas of freedom and family motoring were advertised in sales material such as this 1929 Morris brochure, extolling the Morris car 'for Happiness'.

The *Morris Owner* was the magazine for owners of Morris cars, the first commercial journal produced by a British motor company. Inside there were not only articles about Morris products but also tips on other motoring issues and hints on motor travel. An ambitious young journalist, Miles Thomas, who was later to become vice-chairman at Morris, was put in charge of the project and millions of copies had been printed by the time of the Second World War.

The export market was essential to the Morris business. Separate brochures were produced to promote 'cars for the world'.

(Reprinted from THE DAILY HERALD, 13th January, 1931)

MY SPIN IN THE £100 CAR

Cheap—and good—motoring at last

"THE prospect of cheaper motoring is of intense interest to thousands of *Daily Herald* readers.

"It was, therefore, as their 'personal representative' that I came here to be one of the first to drive Sir William Morris's £100 New Year 'Baby.'

"What can I tell you after having spent the whole day in putting this £100 marvel through its paces?

"Four years ago this same car could not have been produced for twice the price.

GOOD SPEED

"Our motorcar kings have had before them, ever since the birth of the automobile, the attraction of a motorcar that should sell for those magic figures—£100. But none succeeded, though in 1906 a 100-guinea model was produced.

"Then Sir William Morris, the genius of the motor industry, set to work.

"There are two things which amaze me about this new 'baby'—officially known as the Morris Minor S.V. Twoseater. One is its speed on the road and the other its most complete equipment.

"My sole criticism of the car is that Sir William has only fitted a 60 m.p.h. speedometer—and one that will 'clock' 80 is needed!

"Except in 'baby' racing cars, usually supercharged models, I have never done more than a genuine 50 in any 'baby' car—though I am not saying it cannot be done. But the new Morris simply flashed up to 55, and I was afraid that the speedometer needle would move right off the dial

Off for a run in the £100 car.

"I held 55 m.p.h. for half a mile (timed speed), and on a suitable road the 'baby' would do 60, I feel certain.

"Many motorists do not want this high speed, of course, but it does go to show what really extraordinary acceleration the car has—and every driver wants that.

"The equipment is as complete as any car costing three times the price. There are no 'extras' for the owner to obtain. Licence holder, dashlamp, windscreen wiper, driving mirror, and shock absorbers on all four wheels are all included.

"This £100 car is one succession of surprises. I received the first when I got into it. I touch the six-foot mark,

and accordingly I twisted myself up —having had experience with other 'babies'—as I clambered in, for the hood was erected.

SURPRISES

"Judge of my pleasure, then, when I found myself at the wheel without having even knocked my hat off!

"I found I could sit bolt upright with plenty of leg room and without touching the hood with my hat. The single-panel Triplex windscreen gives a clear view of the whole road, and the side curtains make it an extremely cosy car in winter.

"Then I had a whole bunch of surprises. First it was the easy gear

change—'hree-speed and reverse—and then the wonderful way the little car held the road.

"I 'chased' the car over some of the worst surfaces that abound near Cowley, but it was a 'limousine' ride all the way. And the cable-operated four-wheel brakes are really worthy of a speedy little car.

"By this time I was on my mettle. 'No £100 car can be as good as this in everything—maybe you are like the curate's egg. I'll try you on some hills—perhaps you have speed without stamina, because you are over-geared,' I said to myself.

"So I carried on for a few miles until we came to a famous 'trials' hill that, a couple of years ago, unseated half the motorcycle entry and stopped 30 out of 40 cars in a reliability trial.

'PEDIGREE' MOTOR

"It is steep, with a sharp corner, and, in winter time, very, very muddy.

"But 'baby' Morris was not to be stopped. Half-way up we went into second gear, changed into first for the corner, rounded it in style and then changed into second again. We went over the brow at speed.

"And this pedigree car is just as cheap to run as it is to buy. It will cover more than 50 miles to the gallon of petrol, and something like 1500 miles to the gallon of oil.

"On a year's mileage of 10,000— which is about the average—the annual running expenses, including everything, tax, insurance, garage and tyres, should not exceed £25—less than 10s. a week.

"Sir William Morris, on behalf of the 'cheaper motoring' devotees, I thank you."

During the 1920s and '30s, the market for cars in Britain was very difficult and Morris was forced to re-think his models and his prices. A radical move to lower the price of the Morris Minor to £100 (the first British car to reach that magical price) not only buoyed his sales but also attracted a good deal of favourable publicity. Morris, of course, made maximum use of this, producing promotional material that reprinted positive press articles.

Reflecting the mass production techniques at the Cowley factory and capturing the tone of 1930s advertising, the Morris car is heralded as 'the perfect product of modern science'.

Another method of promoting the good qualities of the Morris car was by tales of endurance. This Cowley four-seater had travelled from Singapore to London without mishap in 1929.

Above: Just as Morris had established his own publishing company, Cowley was also to have its own film department pioneering the use of this medium as a publicity tool. The Cine Department at Cowley produced mainly promotional films about the factory and its products. Here we see the fleet of vehicles that the well-organised film department operated in 1936.

Right: Films were frequently shown to distributors and workers alike at film evenings. Here, projectionist Mr Smith shows a film using a Kalee projector.

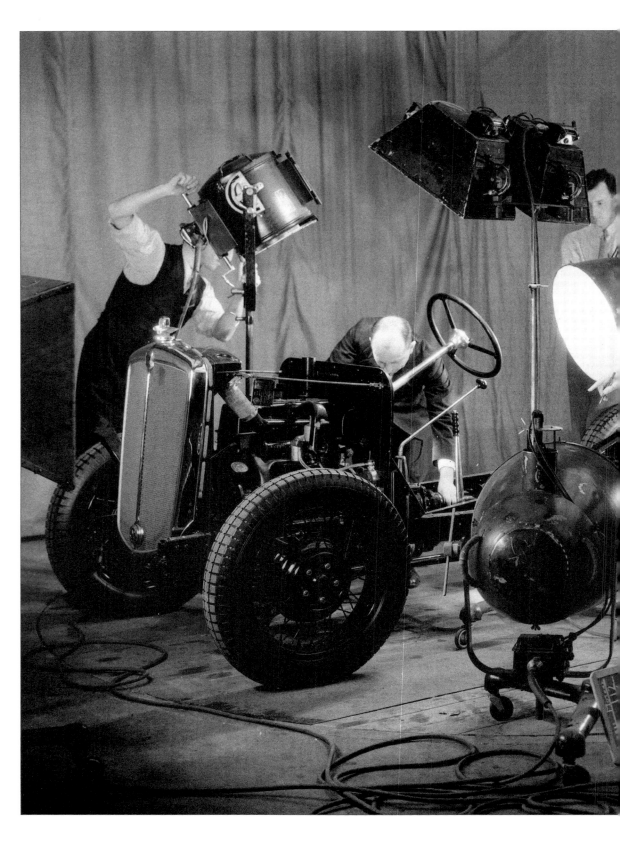

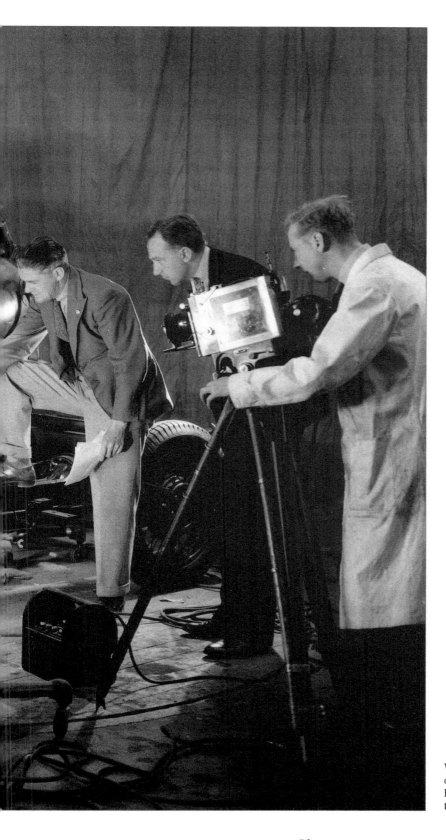

William Morris himself could often be seen in the films. Here the studio is set up for the latest car promotion.

A trip to Cowley was as much a part of a tour to Oxford as the University. This 1938 poster emphasises the company at the expense of any other attraction, and doubtless the company hoped to find some new customers by impressing them with the magnificence of the works.

CHAPTER FIVE

AWAY FROM THE PRODUCTION LINE

The Pressed Steel technique lent itself to the production of other steel products. One of the more well-known names is the Prestcold fridge, seen in many kitchens during the 1940s.

Many workers were employed away from the car assembly lines at Cowley, in other occupations equally vital to the production of the motor car. Essential services included laboratory testing of new materials and the maintenance of machines and equipment. There was much work to be done in the office areas, from the administration of the company, keeping communications flowing and the processing of orders, to the organisation of Cowley's employees. Other products were manufactured at Cowley too, such as the iron lung and the Prestcold fridge.

Life away from work did not necessarily mean life away from Cowley. At a time when the attraction of television and the home computer did not exist, much of an employee's leisure time was also spent at the factory. The provision of recreational activities was seen as an essential part of encouraging a productive workforce. It promoted a sense of community and pride at working for the company.

The range of pursuits was broad, from sport to drama. Football, rugby, cricket, hockey, fishing and athletics were all catered for and regular opportunities were available for competition, both within Cowley and between Morris Motors, Pressed Steel and other companies. William Morris even provided the company with its own athletics ground complete with a fine club house.

If sport was not to one's taste, the Morris Motors Band might attract the musically inclined. The Band was formed under the direction of Morris himself and he always took a keen interest in its success. Club room activities such as billiards or snooker were provided as well as a drama group for those with a theatrical bent.

The welfare and safety of the workforce were also catered for. Early in the 1920s a volunteer fire brigade was formed in the factory. Training and drill were taken very seriously and regular competitions were held to test the aptitude of the firemen and brigades.

Health was another concern. As well as Budd's manufacturing techniques, Pressed Steel adopted his welfare practices and built a hospital in the works in 1926. All types of ailment could be treated, mild or severe. Adjacent was a dentist's surgery, open to all workers in the hope that attention to oral hygiene would keep them away from their jobs for the minimum length of time. Similar facilities were provided at the Morris factories. Fitness was encouraged and there was a selection of health and beauty classes. Even sun-lamp treatment was available!

William Morris (by now Lord Nuffield) always nurtured a deep interest in medical science. In 1938 he visited the Nuffield medical departments at the University where he was shown, among other things, a film about artificial respiration featuring the Both respirator, more commonly known as the 'iron lung'. Seeing the need for such machines in hospitals, he began a programme to build the iron lung at Cowley and, by mass producing them, he was also able to lower the cost to one-quarter of its previous figure. When the war stopped their production, more than 1,700 iron lungs had been made.

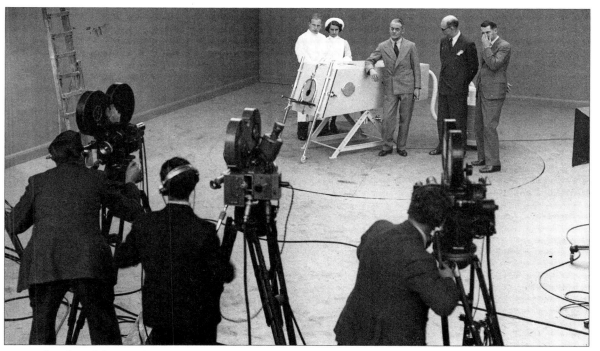

Morris distributed the iron lungs free-of-charge to hospitals who applied for them. Here, the film unit captures the moment as Lord Nuffield himself makes a presentation in 1938.

Before materials reached the production lines, they were checked to make sure they were of the correct quality. Here timber is examined to ensure that it is properly seasoned.

With such a large factory site it was inevitable that parts must be moved around. In 1930 a number of these three-wheeled Reliance tugs were used to move small components about, in this case axles and chassis parts.

The works functioned around the clock. Here cars are despatched during the night hours.

Morris cars were exported around the world. Cars were crated in wooden cases, some components having first been removed and packed separately so that the car could continue its journey by ship without damage. During 1931, when this photograph was taken, more than 3,000 cars were exported by Morris.

The factory also had its own repair shop, seen here in 1928 with a number of cars receiving attention.

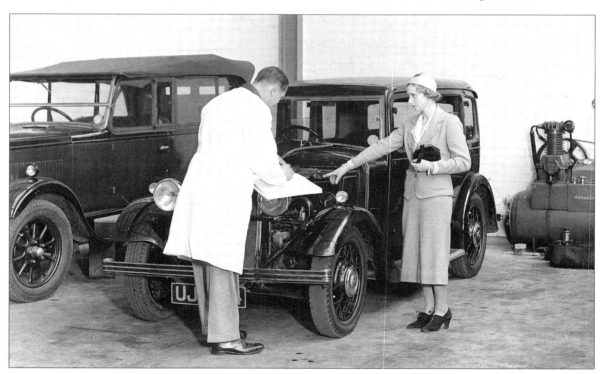

A customer checks over her car with the service engineer.

The service department handled many vehicles, and a small office of staff maintained the index card system used to track the work of the department.

A rather atmospheric photograph from 1923 – Cowley had a test laboratory to analyse materials of all sorts used in motor car production

I.M. (1926) Ltd.—609.

CHEMICAL & PHYSICAL TEST REPORT

MISCELLANEOUS MATERIAL.

LABORATOR
REPORT
NUMBER

3491.

CHEMICAL ANALYSIS:

DESCRIPTION	SPECIFICATION	Viscosity @			Flash point.	Spec. grav.	Sap. value.	Cold pour point
		70°F.	140°F.	200°F.				
Oil.Lub. M.T.	Thin.(Ex RAF)	960	140	58	390°F	.878	1.8	+ 8°c) +46°f)
IDEAL SPECIFICATION.		2000 or less.	–	65 or more	375°F or more	.910 or less.		+35°f or less.

REMARKS: This is a good quality oil but is rather thin, and

at the same time has a very high setting point

(+ 46°f) which would give difficulty in starting

in cold weather.

Date 10.6.28   Signature "E.C. Dickinson."

One of the products tested in the laboratory was new oil. The card report indicates that this oil is not up to the required standard.

The Cashier's Office at Cowley, 1928.

Using the most up-to-date machines – an office calculator in 1936.

The preparation of wage packets for the thousands of workers was a laborious process, alleviated only slightly by these automatic wage dispensing machines, seen here in 1925.

The employees' favourite day of the week? Collecting wages on a pay day in 1937.

Keeping the communications at Cowley alive, three telephonists operate the factory switchboard in 1944.

A Cowley Commissionaire sends a message using the elaborate message chutes that were actuated by compressed air. Morris had a policy of employing some of the many people disabled in the First World War.

Choose a chicken, any chicken! A fabulous display of poultry awaiting the 1929 Christmas draw. In this era, chicken was a luxury, not an everyday food.

The works canteen provided sustenance for the workforce. The poster on the right-hand side of this 1925 photograph advertises the Morris Motors Band's next concert at Oxford Town Hall.

Not only did the canteen provide food, it advertised it as well, in this case a comprehensive display of Australian produce, good British Empire fare. Australia was a favourite holiday destination of William Morris himself.

A well-trained fire brigade was essential for Cowley, not only to protect the workforce but also to minimise risk to the large stocks tied up in the factory. The fire brigade regularly took part in fire competitions against rival factory fire brigades, not just for fun but also to keep the men well prepared. Here, members of the brigade pose proudly with a new trophy in 1929.

William Morris was inspirational in creating the Morris Motors Band. Over many years the band was very successful, winning many competitions.

The football field was where one found many a Cowley worker in his free time. The team from Pressed Steel pose for the camera in 1936.

Inter-departmental rivalry was always a feature of factory social life. The winners of the 1925 tug-of-war competition from the Morris Motors Carpentry department proudly sit with the rope and the victor's trophy.

Above: Morris realised that the welfare of his employees was important if they were to give of their best. The Morris Employment Benefit Scheme provided them with a life assurance policy.

Right: Sport was always taken seriously at Cowley. An annual feature was the sports meeting, held at the playing fields on Crescent Road, adjacent to the original factory and where the athletics pavilion was sited. From 1930 the Athletics and Social Club had a magnificent club house, provided by Sir William Morris himself. This colourful souvenir programme dates from 1925.

Aerobic exercise is no new thing: the Morris Motors health and beauty club in 1930.

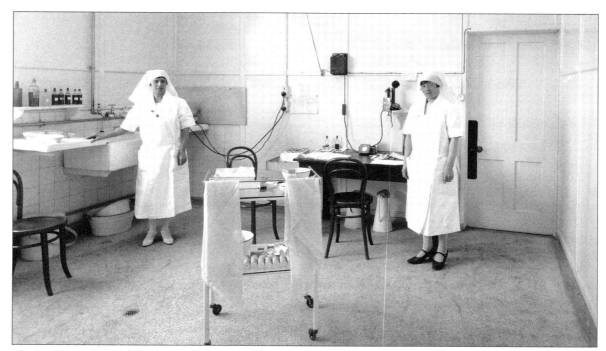

The health of the workforce was also essential to the well-being of the factory. At the surgery, two nurses await the next patient in 1930.

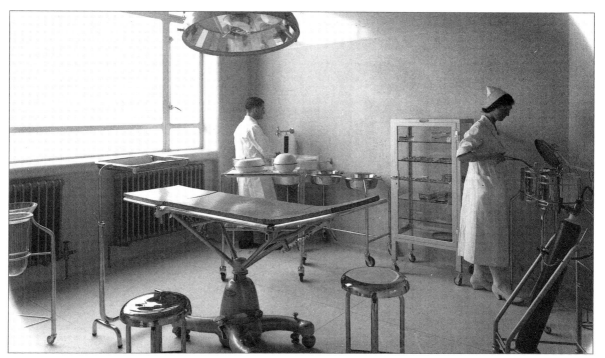

The hospital on the Pressed Steel factory site in 1939, which could treat both minor and major ailments in the fully equipped medical rooms.

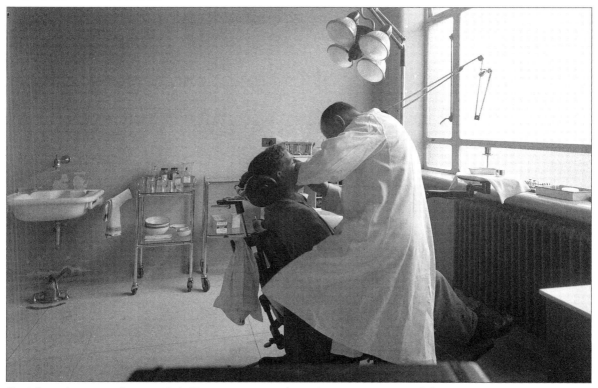

Dental services were also provided. Having an on-site dentist's surgery minimised the time an employee needed to be away from his work.

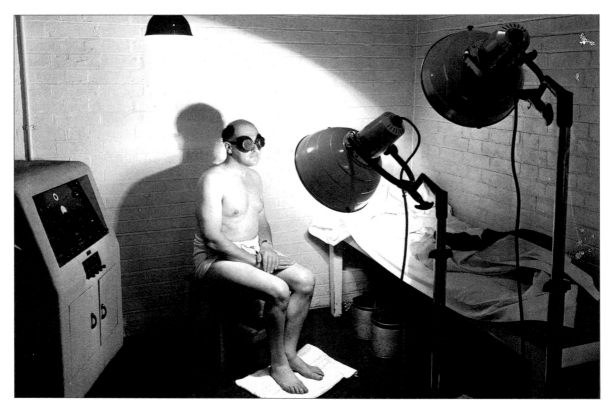

The war period was thought to have had a serious effect on the vitality of the population. In an attempt to revive the pallid workforce, employees were invited to have sun-lamp therapy. The treatment looks rather intimidating for this factory worker in 1946.

A broad range of activities was available on the social side of factory life, such as entertainment in the club games room, which is being utilised by this snooker player at the Morris Radiators Branch.

If sport wasn't to one's liking then maybe a bit of drama was. The Morris Radiators staff display their acting talents in their 1959 production of *Sailor Beware*.

An important part of the sports club was the socialising afterwards. Here the Morris Radiators Branch cricket team members enjoy the annual cricket dinner in 1953.

Perhaps if one wanted a quieter time, a spot of fishing might please you. The Morris Radiators Branch fishing club compete for the T.E. Rees Fishing Cup in 1964.

CHAPTER SIX

SECOND WORLD WAR

*From 1942 tanks were produced at Cowley in the buildings of Morris Industries Exports (later
Nuffield Exports). The Crusader tanks weighed 24 tons and carried six-pounder guns. Almost
650 tanks had been assembled by the end of hostilities.*

The Second World War represented another challenge for the Cowley works. Motor car production was almost immediately stopped and cars already in production were completed and turned over to the war effort. The car factory was a natural place to produce war supplies and Cowley was no exception.

Cowley produced a great range of munitions and fighting machines and virtually every area in the North Works was turned over to war production. The main assembly building, 'C' block, was used as a military inspection area. The recently reorganised 'G'-'K'-'N' block produced mines, trucks and light reconnaissance vehicles. Wings for the Horsa glider were made in the sawmill area, De Havilland wing units were constructed in 'B' block and power units for Lancaster bombers and Beaufighter aeroplanes came out of the office buildings in 'L' block.

In preparation for the war, new buildings were constructed to the south of the North Works on the other side of Garsington Road. These buildings were primarily concerned with aeroplane salvage, repair and manufacture. The 50 Maintenance Unit transported damaged aircraft to Cowley, where they were stored next to 'R' block and then transferred to 'S' block for repair or recycling by the Civilian Repair Unit. In the same block, complete Tiger Moth aeroplanes were manufactured, one of the first examples of aeroplanes being produced using mass production techniques. Indeed, the flow technique was the cornerstone of Cowley's war production as it was for peacetime car production. Almost any war supply, from torpedoes to tanks, could be manufactured speedily using assembly line techniques.

On the north side of Garsington Road, Morris Industries Exports (MIE) began to produce Crusader tanks from 1942. The 24-ton Crusaders were assembled from 10,000 components and took a week to produce. Later, MIE also produced the large armoured amphibious craft called 'Neptune'.

More than three-quarters of the regular Cowley workforce was called away for active service. Nevertheless, the workforce at Cowley during the war years swelled to over 10,000, more than double the peacetime number. A great proportion of that number was women, one of the more notable being Winston Churchill's daughter, Sarah, who was engaged in the production of brass shell casings.

During the Second World War, a number of schemes were tried to combat petrol rationing. One idea was to fit cars with coal gas or 'producer gas' systems. The gas was stored in a rather cumbersome bag that was fitted to the roof of the vehicle, in this case a Morris Ten.

Wartime meant factory production was turned over to the war effort. Among the items produced at Cowley were armoured personnel carriers. In 1940 a train-load of carriers awaits departure from the factory.

Once again women were brought back to mainstream factory jobs during wartime. Here the turret section of a Crusader tank is assembled.

Sir Miles Thomas triumphantly drives the first tank out of the factory on 8 May 1942. The tank was assembled from some 10,000 parts and took twelve days to put together.

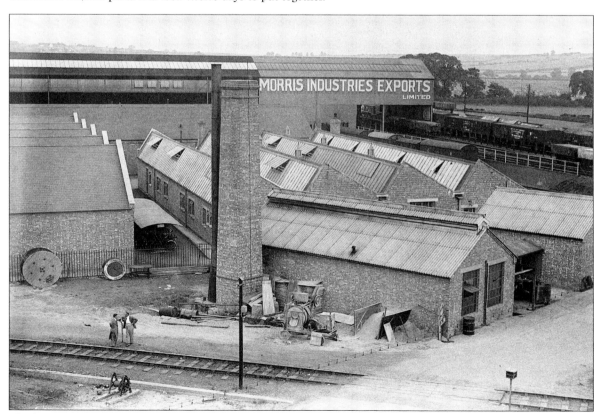

The home of tank production at Cowley – the Morris Industries Exports building.

Other small military vehicles were produced at Cowley, such as this small amphibious armoured car, known as the Salamander. The vehicle is being tested in a water bath at Cowley in 1942.

The company designed and built an amphibious carrier, the *Neptune*, capable of carrying up to 5 tons and accommodating a 17-pounder anti-tank gun and travelling at a rate of 5 knots. It is seen here on test at the lake at Blenheim Palace.

Alec Issigonis is perhaps better known for the Morris Minor or Mini but during the war at Morris, he was engaged in building a variety of unusual military vehicles. One such was this strange 'motorised wheelbarrow', which was designed to be disassembled and airdropped to the troops in the field for local transport.

The first large-scale contract for wartime production at Cowley was for the complete construction of Tiger Moth aircraft. Before the war, traditional methods of construction yielded no more than 200 aeroplanes per year. By applying Morris production methods, Cowley was able to turn out 40 Tiger Moths each week.

The Pressed Steel Company was also involved with aeroplane manufacture. Here two men assemble the fuselage of an aircraft.

Morris Radiators Branch (formerly Osberton Radiators) made their own contribution. Here women assemble the cores of radiators for aircraft.

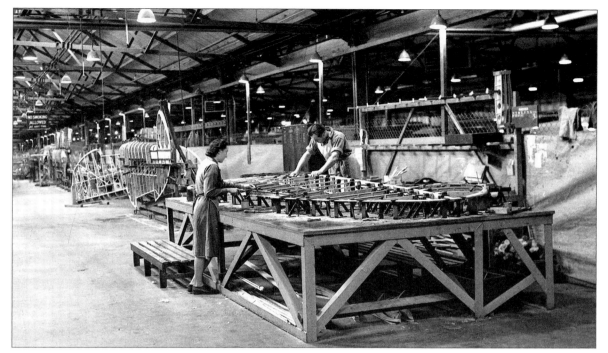

From early in 1942, Cowley was engaged in construction of the tail units of Horsa gliders. Even the time-consuming process of gluing the plywood skin onto the framework of the tail got the Morris treatment. By judicious use of clamps and inflated bicycle inner tubes, the lengthy task of pin-tacking the tail section to hold it in place until the glue had dried was avoided.

The Cowley factory was capable of doing the complete job right up to the final stages of applying camouflage paint.

One of the more interesting aspects of the war effort was the organisation of aircraft repairs. William Morris played a central rôle in this operation, known as the Civilian Repair Organisation, and was for a short time in 1940 responsible for the whole operation. The Organisation comprised

1,500 repair centres or Civilian Repairs Units, of which Cowley was No. 1 Aeroplanes, such as this Hurricane fighter, were salvaged and brought to Cowley where they were stripped and repaired, any components past repair being melted down and used in the production of new parts.

At work in the No. 1 Civilian Repair Unit in 1940. By the end of 1945, it had handled over 75,000 aircraft repairs.

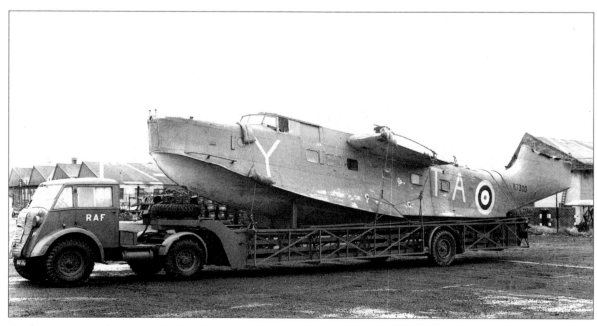

Cowley was not only responsible for the repair of damaged aircraft but also helped to salvage and transport them. The Transport Department was home to the 50 Maintenance Unit, RAF, which was engaged in recovering aeroplanes and taking them to the Repair Units. In this picture, a flying boat arrives at Cowley in 1943 on a 'Queen Mary' trailer.

As in the First World War, standard munitions manufacture was carried out at Cowley. Here torpedoes are being manufactured for supply to the Admiralty.

War production saw many women enter the factory to do jobs previously the reserve of men. One such instance was in the Drawing Office.

A woman at work at the Pressed Steel factory, welding together jerry cans.

Regular displays of war production showed how the Cowley factories supported the war effort. This display of Pressed Steel production gives a small example of more than £3,000,000 worth of war equipment produced in the tool department.

After peace had returned it was time to think about car production again. Here the contents of a Garsington Road store (packaged bumpers) are being examined.

With the war finally over, the remaining parts of wrecked aeroplanes were transported away from Cowley by the RAF and scrapped.

The new model for the post-war period was to be the Morris Minor. In this view the Mosquito, the prototype for the Minor, sits outside the still camouflaged factory in 1944.

CHAPTER SEVEN

POST-WAR BOOM, TAKE-OVER AND MERGER

Morris products were subjected to diverse tests, including particularly severe ones such as this freezing test being carried out on a Morris Minor.

During the war years, the workforce had been higher than ever before. The employment level at Cowley alone had risen to 10,000 and stood at 45,000 for the Nuffield Organisation as a whole. This time, the machinery installed during the war was available for peacetime production.

The car market in Britain immediately after the war was entirely in the control of the country's motor manufacturers. Post-war austerity and the Government's drive to promote exports meant that demand easily outstripped supply. Exports were essential to bring in foreign currency and as demand abroad was just as strong as at home, Morris sought to exploit the situation by setting up foreign assembly plants in countries such as Australia, India and South Africa. By 1950, the level of Morris exports had quadrupled from its immediate pre-war figure. Car production became a contest of speed of manufacture, and Cowley expanded to meet the demand. Lord Nuffield was determined to challenge the renewed competition from American companies.

In 1949 the 'G'-'K'-'N' block was again modernised. Five assembly lines were installed, using skids unique to each model to carry the cars down the track. The 'M' block was given over to producing complete subframes with engines installed. The rebuilding of the block allowed for a 30 per cent increase in output. South Works experienced the biggest expansion of the 1950s. New buildings were erected, initially being used for stores and for the production of CKD (Completely Knocked Down) kits for export. When, a few years later, production of the Morris Minor had increased significantly, one of these buildings was converted into a manufacturing facility. The buildings had originally been constructed with high roofs and this foresight allowed the easy installation of the overhead conveyors necessary for the line.

Arguably the biggest influence on the shape of Cowley in the post-war period came in 1952. Morris had begun to lag behind Austin, who had made a better start to peacetime production, partly because Cowley was not as quick to grasp the latest production techniques. Austin was now headed by one Leonard Lord, the pre-war factory organisation master at Morris, who had left Cowley in 1936 on not-so-friendly terms with Lord Nuffield. In the late 1940s Lord had suggested a merger but Lord Nuffield had not been so keen. In 1952, however, after a number of years of trying, the grand marriage to form the British Motor Corporation (BMC) was effected.

This merger signalled the end of expansion at Cowley, which for a while seemed destined to become the poorer partner to the Austin Longbridge factory. The largest building investment of that new BMC period was 'E' block to the south. It provided for a new paint facility, 'Rotodip' body preparation plant and body store. In 1954 an overhead conveyor was stretched across the Oxford Eastern Bypass, providing a direct connection to the North Works and obviating the need to truck bodies across the road. Fifteen years later, another conveyor spanned the Garsington Road, connecting 'E' block to the North Works. In 1960 the public view of South Works was characterised by the construction of some office blocks close to the road. In 1962 the 'G'-'K'-'N' block was upgraded to semi-automatic lines and equipped with new conveyors to cope with the large Morris Oxford and Mini volumes.

This was to be the last major expansion of the Cowley works.

The resumption of car manufacture after the war was largely based on pre-war models, such as the Morris Eight Series E, until new models were available.

Immediate post-war production was hampered by the difficulties in the supply of components. Here we see a shop full of stockpiled bodies awaiting the arrival of sufficient engines for the chassis.

In the post-war period the national slogan was 'export or die', and the home market was deliberately restricted to concentrate on exports to bring in foreign currency. The Nuffield Organisation therefore turned its eyes to far flung markets such as India and Australia.

The thriving Exports Department packing Morris Minors and Rileys for sale abroad.

Loading transporters with Morris Minors for their journey to the port.

A familiar view at Cowley. Workers leave the factory gates in 1950, the majority still on bicycles just as they were in the 1930s.

The lines flow once again: Morris Minor production in 1950.

Morris' talented chief designer Alec Issigonis, whose post-war Morris Minor design was to be one of the Company's most successful products.

A Morris Minor passing through the paint drying kilns.

One of the most significant investment programmes at Cowley during the 1950s was the building of 'E' block, the last major building at the plant. It housed a new body store, paint shop and the 'Rotodip' body preparation facility, through which this Morris Oxford can be seen passing.

Before despatch, all cars were inspected. Here, Farina-bodied MG Magnettes and Morris Minor vans sit on adjoining lines in 1959.

The wooden-framed Morris Minor Traveller estate car needed vintage production methods. The 'Traveller' part of the car was constructed using pre-war coachbuilding techniques.

Staff training on new products was essential and the service technical school provided regular appraisals of Morris products.

Individual components were also subject to rigorous testing like these Riley engines being put through their paces on test beds.

Above: Although many more operations had become automated, the fitting of trim was still a manual task.

Right: The preparation of trimming materials had also changed very little over the years and was still being machined in the traditional way in this 1952 photograph.

The operation of the vehicles was inspected thoroughly. Here the headlamp beam alignment on a Morris Oxford is checked using a test machine.

Final preparation of bodywork before inspection; paintwork is touched up and polished on Wolseley cars.

So many wheels! Tyres are fitted to the hundreds of wheels required every day for Morris products.

All the right parts in the right place. Conveyors transport all the necessary trim to the exact spot on the line for installation while Riley cars and Morris vans move down adjacent tracks.

A woman at Morris Radiators patiently assembles radiator cores by hand.

Morris Radiators did not just manufacture radiators. This 1960 view shows the hot dipping of ashtrays to chrome-plate them.

NUMBER OF CERTIFICATE 34508

TRANSFER No. VARIOUS.

AMOUNT OF 7½% CUMULATIVE PREFERENCE STOCK

£ 206,477

(REPRESENTED BY UNITS OF £4 EACH)

MORRIS MOTORS LIMITED

INCORPORATED UNDER THE COMPANIES ACTS 1908 TO 1917

AUTHORISED CAPITAL £ 5.650.000.

DIVIDED INTO

£ 3,000,000 SEVEN AND ONE HALF PER CENT CUMULATIVE PREFERENCE STOCK TRANSFERABLE
IN MULTIPLES OF £1 AND £2,650,000 ORDINARY STOCK TRANSFERABLE IN MULTIPLES OF 5/-

THE PREFERENCE STOCK IS ENTITLED TO A FIXED CUMULATIVE PREFERENTIAL DIVIDEND OF 7½ PER CENT PER ANNUM
AND TO PRIORITY AS REGARDS CAPITAL AND DIVIDEND BUT TO NO FURTHER PARTICIPATION IN PROFITS OR ASSETS

This is to Certify that   THE BRITISH MOTOR CORPORATION LIMITED

of   COWLEY, OXFORD

is/are the Registered Proprietors of   TWO HUNDRED AND SIX THOUSAND FOUR
HUNDRED AND SEVENTY SEVEN   Pounds
Seven and One half per cent Cumulative Preference Stock of Morris Motors Limited
subject to the Memorandum and Articles of Association of the said Company

Given under the Common Seal of the Company
this   SIXTH   day of   AUGUST

DIRECTOR

SECRETARY

NOTE THE STOCK IS TRANSFERABLE IN AMOUNTS AND MULTIPLES OF £1
NO TRANSFER OF SUCH STOCK OR ANY PORTION THEREOF WILL BE REGISTERED UNLESS ACCOMPANIED BY THIS CERTIFICATE

1952 was a significant year for Morris Motors when it merged with its great rival, the Austin Motor Company, to form the British Motor Corporation. These certificates were issued to formalise the share transfer between old and new companies.

A scene from the stores in 1960. Manufacturing required the stockpiling of many parts in contrast to the 'just-in-time' philosophy that would be introduced from Japan in the 1990s.

137

For some time the Mini was assembled at both Cowley and Longbridge. The Morris version was known as the Morris Mini-Minor. Here is Mini production in its first year, 1959.

Fifties style! The rear window trim is fitted to a Mini.

At the end of the line. A Mini reaches final inspection.

An 1100 is prepared for the 'Rotodip' facility. A large bar has been inserted through the body so it can be rotated as on a spit during the cleaning and painting processes.

In spite of carrying the names of Austin and Morris, the two versions were not split between the Longbridge and Cowley factories. In this overhead view the first and third cars are Morris Mini-Minors whilst the second and fourth are Austin Se7ens. How does one tell them apart? By the different radiator grilles and bonnet badges.

The 1100's larger brother and another design from Alec Issigonis; an 1800 reaches final assembly in 1966.

A typical office scene in 1965. Regimented rows of desks are presided over by a rather stern-looking office supervisor.

Sixties modern technology. Remote control of the assembly lines using punch cards.

Engine diagnostics. The performance of a Morris Minor engine is monitored using a Crypton tuning machine.

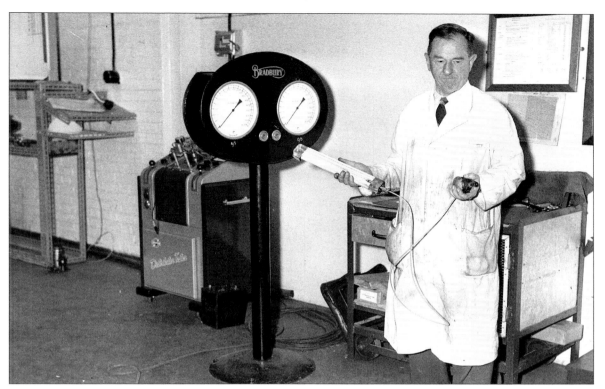

A variety of diagnostic machines was available to this 1961 BMC technician.

Early computing power; the computer room at BMC Service in 1961.

Edward Heath arrives on a visit to Cowley in 1967, rather disappointingly in a Ford.

CHAPTER EIGHT

MECHANISATION: FROM BL TO ROVER

The year is 1975, as is evident from the fashionable hairstyles whose proud owners are undoubtedly wearing flares as they weld components on the line.

More organisational upheaval affected Cowley from the end of the 1960s. BMC, which had two years previously merged with Jaguar, came together with the massive Leyland Corporation to form the British Leyland Motor Corporation (BLMC). The greater strength of Leyland in the partnership resulted in its chairman, Sir Donald Stokes, heading up the new Corporation. For Cowley, this signalled the start of a long rationalisation of the plant. From now on 'Morris' was one marque among the many owned by British Leyland.

During the late 1960s, the Pressed Steel main assembly building was reorganised and a large part given over to the production of bodies for the Austin Maxi, Britain's first five-door hatchback car. In spite of new production systems, cutbacks faced the factory during the mid-seventies. The Ryder Report of 1975 recommended a wide-ranging restructuring of British Leyland's operations. Production continued with models such as the Morris Marina, which was in time replaced by the Ital. This model, discontinued in the mid-eighties, was the last car to bear the Morris name.

In 1977 the new man at the top of British Leyland, Michael Edwardes, brought in more swingeing changes. Cowley became part of the Austin Morris Group and the overmanned factory had its workforce slimmed down. Still British Leyland was struggling and Edwardes made the decision to undertake a joint venture with the Japanese Honda company. The first fruit of this was to be built at Cowley, and the Triumph Acclaim joined the Rover SD1 and the Austin Ambassador in the 'G'-'K'-'N' block. The advent of Austin-Rover in 1982 brought new models and new technology, including more automation of the lines and computer-aided design.

In 1986 the Rover 800 replaced the SD1. The new line employed several interesting modern processes. One was the rather crudely termed 'stuff-up' operation, whereby complete engine units were installed into the car from underneath. Another was the 'DODO' procedure (Doors On Doors Off), where doors were attached to the cars and then removed halfway down the line, from whence they travelled separately to an overhead trim facility before being re-attached further along the line.

By 1990, British Leyland had become Rover Group and this era was to see the most significant changes to the Cowley landscape since the original growth of the factory in the 1930s and '40s. The manufacturing facilities were to be rationalised under the Cowley consolidation programme. The reorganisation marked the end for the North and the South Works blocks. Production was moved completely to the former Pressed Steel site to the east of the Oxford Eastern Bypass, this being the most cost-effective way of reorganising the plant, eliminating the need to move the heaviest of the machinery.

In 1992 the last two main models assembled in the South Works, the Maestro and Montego, were transferred to the main 'A' building. The legacy of the Pressed Steel days, a myriad of production lines for producing bodies for each of its different customers, was swept away. In the new plant, raw materials occupied one end of the plant, body manufacture followed by painting took place in the middle areas, and vehicle assembly and despatch came last. Throughout 1998 and 1999 an investment of over £700 million by Rover Group's new owners, BMW, brought to the Cowley assembly areas the latest in technology. The launch of the Rover '75' was to take slimmed-down Cowley, now renamed 'Rover Oxford', into the next century.

From 1993 both the North and South Works buildings were demolished and open land returned. The conveyors that once crossed the roads have disappeared, replaced by new industrial units. A supermarket occupies the site to the south-east of the roundabout at the junction of Garsington Road and the Bypass, where traffic is now hurried past on a fly-over. The motorist may glance to one side and be reminded of Pressed Steel by the survival of its clock tower and offices, which still overlook the road as they did in the 1930s.

Even the original factory, the Military College, has not escaped despite being a listed building. Though recognisable from the outside, the interior has been converted into elegant flats. The residents can look out of their new homes and see the same view that William Morris once saw as he gazed out of his office window over the empty allotments dreaming of the mighty industry which he was to shape on that soil.

The master of British Leyland. Sir Donald Stokes, head of Leyland Motors, became the chief of the new British Leyland Motor Corporation (BLMC) following Leyland's merger with British Motor Holdings Ltd (itself a merger between BMC and Jaguar).

As British Leyland began to struggle in the early 1970s it introduced new models in an attempt to boost its performance. Here windscreens are being fitted into the Morris Marina.

Morris Marina bodies, produced by Pressed Steel Fisher, glide rather mysteriously towards their next coat of paint.

The spick and span office of the new BLMC Service department in 1968.

The hub of the computer network was the 'Gerber' room, which contained computer readout machines.

New design methods; 'Computer Aided Design' being used to design tools at Pressed Steel Fisher in 1980.

The last Maxi body reaches the end of the line at Pressed Steel Fisher in 1981.

An historic moment. Michael Edwardes and Mr Kawashima shake hands on the BL–Honda deal in 1979. The first project would be the Cowley-built Triumph Acclaim.

Welding bodies for the Triumph Acclaim in 1981.

On the assembly line. Engines for the Acclaim are installed from underneath the car.

The first result of Anglo-Japanese collaboration; the finished Triumph Acclaim.

Computerised control of the Maestro assembly line helped to monitor the automatic body framing station.

Look – no hands. Mass production methods reached their peak with the Maestro line, which was equipped with fourteen robots capable of welding five different body styles. More than 60 per cent of the spot welds on the body were applied by a robot.

In at the deep end. A Maestro body descends into the electrostatic dip tank, giving it a coat of corrosion resistant paint.

The automatic framing station putting together the body assembly of a Rover 800. Everything from positioning to welding was now done automatically.

By 1992 even the fitting of windscreen glass was completed without manual assistance.

The changing face of Cowley. By the beginning of the 1990s, the old factory was becoming unsuitable for the installation of the most up-to-date production methods and redevelopment was decided upon. This picture shows the start of the demolition of North Works in 1993.

Like monuments to the production line, body conveyors remain standing above the demolition.

The new face of Cowley. A Tesco supermarket stands where once was the Sales Despatch building on the south-east side of the Garsington Road.

Anonymous but neat industrial units replace the mish-mash of factory buildings that had grown up over eighty years.

A new era of production at Cowley. Representing a £700 million investment, the modern production lines for the Rover '75' model were some of the most advanced in the world.

The Rover '75' represented Cowley's new large car for the twenty-first century.

APPENDIX

LIST OF BMIHT NEGATIVE NUMBERS

The photographs in this book are taken from the archives of the Heritage Motor Centre. Enquiries about our photographic services are welcome. If you wish to make an enquiry about any of the photographs reproduced in this volume it will be of great assistance if you quote the negative number from the list below.

Page No.	Year	Neg. No.	Page No.	Year	Neg. No.	Page No.	Year	Neg. No.
			37t	1926	C-1629	68t	1929	C-7806
1	1949	C-25771	37b	1925	C-056	68b	1932	PS-499
2	1957	C-76597	38t	1926	C-1144A	69t	1929	PS-164
3	1924	C-609	38b	1929	C-7694	69b	1927	C-2049
4	1929	C-7679	39t	1926	C-1626	70t	1934	C-14257
5	1959	C-87962	39b	1929	C-7540	70b	1939	C-20481
6	1960	H6025	40/41	1926	C-1624			
			42t	1929	C-7679	Chapter Four		
Introduction			42b	1929	C-8247	71	1923	C-561
8	1927	C-1684	43t	1926	C-1623	73t	1929	C-8211
9t	1919	C-31567	43b	1929	C-8338	73b	1950	C-35744
9b	1914	TUR-445	44t	1932	C-10829	74t	1924	C-399
10t	1921	C-22944	44b	1928	C-7357	74b	1926	C-1246
10b	1966	C-165836	45	1930	C-8478	75t	1926	C-975A
11t	c. 1975	–	46t	1926	C-03	75b	1924	C-490
11b	1986	C-326930	46b	1930	C-8869	76t	1938	C-18313
12/13	1934	C-13036	47t	1933	C-12055	76b	1938	C-18271
14t	1924	C-609	47b	1926	C-1613	77t	1929	C-7732
14b	1926	C-056	48t	1929	C-8328	77b	1929	C-7589
15t	1928	C-7265	48b	1930	C-9196	78t	1926	C-1243
15b	1933	C-12660	49	1926	–	78b	1929	–
16t	1939	C-20163	50t	1927	–	79	1931	–
16b	1944	C-23785	50b	1928	C-6080	80t	1929	C-8277
17t	1954	C-56469	51t	1928	C-063	80b	1929	C-7747
17b	1954	C-54586	51b	c. 1930	–	81t	1936	C-16245
18	1960	C-91430	52/53	1934	C-14083	81b	1931	C-10619
			54t	1934	C-13435	82/83	1933	C-12547
Chapter One			54b	1936	C-16075	84	1938	C-18758
19	c. 1907	C-20814	55t	1939	C-20042			
22t	c. 1896	C-59046	55b	1937	C-17398	Chapter Five		
22b	c. 1909	C-32456	56/57	1938	C-18432	85	1940	PS-1351
23	c. 1895	–	58	1935	–	87t	1939	C-19952
24t	1903	C-24231				87b	1938	C-19376
24b	1912	C-51984				88t	1933	C-12881
25	1913	C-24162	Chapter Three			88b	1930	C-8532
26t	1913	C-8205	59	1925	C-059	89t	1926	C-1051
26b	1913	–	61	1933	C-12073	89b	1931	C-10460
27t	1914	–	62t	1929	C-7680	90t	1928	C-7008
27b	1914	–	62b	1927	C-66223	90b	1937	C-17607
28	1916	C-91644	63t	1926	C-056	91t	1928	C-4038
29t	c. 1917	C-97387	63b	1933	C-12061	91b	1923	C-03
29b	c. 1917	C-97387	64t	1926	C-1615	92t	1928	C-7771
30/31	1918	C-039	64bl	1930	C-8784	92b	1928	C-7126
32t	1918	C-3006	64br	1930	PS-277	93t	1936	C-16307
32b	1919	C-73813	65t	1926	C-1291	93b	1925	C-495A
			65b	1938	PS-1213	94t	1937	C-17560
Chapter Two			66	1933	PS-570	94b	1944	C-23765
33	1924	C-412	67t	1933	PS-573	95t	1936	C-16308
36	1928	C-5023	67b	1932	PS-484	95b	1929	C-8353

Page No.	Year	Neg. No.	Page No.	Year	Neg. No.	Page No.	Year	Neg. No.
96t	1925	C-822	117t	1944	C-23517	139t	1959	C-88592
96b	1928	C-7390	117b	1944	C-23770	139b	1968	C-184929
97t	1929	C-8077	118	1943	PS-1803	140	1965	C-128259
97b	1926	C-012	119t	1945	PS-2071	141t	1966	C-164903
98t	1936	PS-958	119b	1944	C-23772	141b	1965	C-161338
98b	1925	C-744	120t	1946	C-24685	142t	1960	C-96771
99t	1935	–	120b	1944	C-23554	142b	1961	C-100635
99b	1925	C-71574				143t	1961	C-100636
100t	c. 1930	C-298163	Chapter Seven			143b	1961	C-101735
100b	1930	–	121	1949	C-32914	144	1967	C-79214
101t	1939	C-19504	123	1946	C-25248			
101b	1946	PS-2446	124t	1946	C-24542	Chapter Eight		
102t	1946	C-25133	124b	1949	C-29465	145	1975	C-255199
102b	1954	C-54930	125t	1948	C-28700	148t	1968	C-190705
103t	1959	C-89947	125b	1951	C-39943	148b	1971	C-215677
103b	1953	C-52504	126t	1950	C-35087	149t	1971	C-210669
104	1964	C-123443	126b	1950	C-34611	149b	1968	C-184187
			127	1946	C-25277B	150t	1976	C-270590
Chapter Six			128t	1958	C-82019	150b	c. 1980	–
105	1944	C-23256	128b	1949	C-29352	151t	1981	C-311787
107	1939	C-20731	129t	1959	C-85829	151b	1979	–
108t	c. 1940	C-102794	129b	1966	C-164762	152t	1981	C-312629
108b	1942	C-22628	130t	1948	C-27378	152b	1981	C-312626
109t	1942	C-22330	130b	1948	C-27624	153t	1981	C-312750
109b	1937	C-7614	131t	1948	C-27783	153b	1983	C-319204
110t	1942	C-22344	131b	1952	C-44245	154t	1983	C-320827
110b	1945	C-23984	132t	1951	C-42776	154b	1983	C-319174
111t	1944	C-23388	132b	1954	C-54220	155t	1986	C-44986c
111b	1943	C-23100	133t	1955	C-62074	155b	1992	C9206255
112t	1940	PS-1425	133b	1956	C-65829	156t	1993	TUR-241
112b	1943	C-22810	134/135	1949	C-25771	156b	1993	TUR-278
113t	1943	C-23046	136	1960	C-95855	157t	1994	TUR-450
113b	1939	C-20726	137t	1952	–	157b	1998	TUR-583
114/115	1940	C-21452	137b	1960	C-94749	158t	1998	–
116t	1940	C-21016	138t	1959	C-87962	158b	1998	–
116b	1941	C-22082	138b	1959	C-88782			